IS BANKRUPTCY FOR YOU?

The Easy-to-Read Guide to Understanding Personal Bankruptcy

Mark R. Schottler, JD MBA

www.schottlerbankruptcylaw.com/is-bankruptcy-for-you

708-316-1839

Serving the Greater Chicagoland Area.

ISBN-13: 978-0692555446
ISBN-10: 0692555447

Published in the United States.

Printed by CreateSpace.

TABLE OF CONTENTS

PREFACE

I strongly believe in the power of bankruptcy and what it can do to change your life. After almost twenty years as a consumer bankruptcy lawyer, I decided to write this book to explain what bankruptcy actually is, how it works and why it matters to not only to us as individuals but to society and the economy as a whole. Although I also practice in other areas of law, my first job as an attorney was as a Bankruptcy Lawyer and I have been doing it each and every day since.

"What exactly is bankruptcy?" I am asked that question constantly, as soon as I tell people what I do for a living. I am asked this question by my friends and neighbors, by parents at my kids' soccer games and even by other attorneys who do not practice it. Everyone has heard of the term but very few know what it is or how it works. I hope to change that with this book.

Throughout this book, I talk about why I believe bankruptcy matters. At its core, bankruptcy is about money owed, and as many people know, household debt is at an all-time high. Debt causes stress on individuals and their families. The stress from debt can come to consume every part of your life. I will show you the relief bankruptcy can provide for the individual who files and the incredible transformations I have seen in my clients over the last twenty years. I also give my take on why bankruptcy is relevant for the economy and society as a whole. I believe that the recent recession and economic downturn have made consumer bankruptcy more important than ever.

I have laid out the book in this format:

- **What consumer bankruptcy is and what it is not.**

I have written this to give a basic understanding of how regular people can use bankruptcy protection in their everyday lives. I say consumer (or individual) bankruptcy, as I will no more than briefly touch on corporate bankruptcy. In this book, I do talk about the best routes for small businesses to take in bankruptcy but do not get into big business bankruptcies. The subject of corporate restructuring for larger companies is extremely complex and very detailed.

- **Practical aspects of filing a bankruptcy case.**

I lay out a discussion of when you should file for bankruptcy. I will attempt to dispel some of the myths about bankruptcy and more importantly try to cut through the propaganda and negative information that has come to surround it and its use. I will also discuss each type of bankruptcy case and how and why an individual might use each one. I will touch on the requirements to file and what each type of case will achieve for the person who files. I will lay out in some detail what you can expect before, during and after the filing for individual bankruptcy. While the information in this section is no substitute for a good bankruptcy lawyer, it will hopefully explain the basics of bankruptcy practice and give a better understanding as to what you can expect if you go through it. In this section I will also talk about the bankruptcy choices small business and small business owners have available to them.

- **US Bankruptcy Code and how recent changes can be used by individuals.**

I include tips to help you prepare for filing your case and for managing your case as it proceeds through the court system. These tips are merely suggestions and should not be taken as a substitute for good legal advice. The changes to the bankruptcy laws in 2005 made it so complex that a good lawyer is an absolute necessity to navigate the ins and outs of the system and achieve maximum results.

I also share stories from my own practice as well as interesting information about current and newsworthy bankruptcy events. Most interestingly, I have included examples of *twenty celebrities* who have filed for bankruptcy to show you that bankruptcy is out there and more common than you might think. These are people in the public spotlight who chose bankruptcy for its swift action and powerful results to put their lives back on track. The examples are there to show you it can work for you, too.

I hope you will find the book to be both interesting and helpful in understanding what bankruptcy is, what it does and why it is so very relevant in our lives today. I believe in the power of bankruptcy to change your life because I have seen it firsthand.

Chapter One: What is Bankruptcy?

A very basic definition of bankruptcy is that it is a federal law that sets out legal procedures that allow an individuals and corporations to eliminate some or all of debts they owe. Thus, the idea of bankruptcy is very simple: follow a set of legal procedures and your debts will be eliminated in whole or in part. Sounds easy in theory. Unfortunately it is not that simple in practice.

Bankruptcy laws have been around for a long time and have become more and more complicated over the years. The procedures for filing bankruptcy have become so complex that most non-bankruptcy lawyers generally refuse to handle a bankruptcy case, but will instead refer it to an attorney with a primary practice in the area. It is now almost impossible for an individual to file on their own.

The reason the bankruptcy laws have become so complicated is that the people and companies who lend money want to make it harder and harder to file. These people are called your "creditors." Creditor just means someone you owe money. Creditors want to make filing for bankruptcy more difficult because they want to get paid. Filing not only eliminates all or part of your debt, but it also takes away their power or position of strength. Think of any time you have taken out a loan: the lender made all the rules for repayment and set the terms based on a credit score and credit report that you have little control over (and may not even be accurate). The lenders give the borrower very little choice. Bankruptcy changes that.

Celebrity Bankruptcy Spotlight

50 Cent, rapper: After being sued over an alleged sex tape and losing, rapper Curtis James Jackson III, better known as 50 Cent, declared bankruptcy in July of 2015.

Chapter Two: Should I File Bankruptcy?

How do you know if or when you should file for bankruptcy? The answer is different for each person and it is unique to his or her individual situation. Deciding to file for bankruptcy involves many factors. Financial as well as emotional factors are often involved as part of the process. If you are thinking about filing for bankruptcy, do the following:

1. Define the nature of your problem.
2. Determine how bankruptcy will help you.
3. Determine if you even qualify to file.

1. Defining the Problem

The first step in considering bankruptcy is taking stock of your own situation. Review your monthly income and monthly expenses. Determine if you are having trouble "making ends meet" each and every month. For example, if your household net take-home pay (after taxes and insurance) is about $2,500 per month, with rent/mortgage and groceries of $1,800 per month, even the minimum payments on $10,000 of credit card debt will not leave you with enough to live on.

Next, try to determine how much you actually owe. In many cases, people do not know the full extent of their debt. This can stem from fear and stress arising from the situation of being in debt. The thought of sorting out your finances can make you upset or even scared. This level of stress is a sign you may need help with your financial problems. Gather all of your important papers and write up what you owe to each debt.

Finally, envision where you want to be in the future. I always tell my clients to picture where they want to go and then to make a two-year plan, a five-year plan and a ten-year plan to get there. These plans don't have to be perfect or detailed. Just a road map of how you want your life to be. If the future you see does not include the stress of being in debt, then it is time to consider filing for bankruptcy.

2. Determine How Bankruptcy Can Help You.

As a strictly financial decision, you should file for bankruptcy when you are unable to pay bills as they come due. This means that the payments on your debt exceed your income after paying those things necessary for day to day life. This is very common with bankruptcies involving credit card and medical debts. Look at your use of credit and see if you are using loans and credit cards for everyday expenses. If you are using debt to make ends meet, or if you are just making the minimums (or have been unable to even make payments), you are probably ready to file. Filing bankruptcy completely eliminates these types of debts.

Another financial situation that is an indication that you should file for personal bankruptcy is when a collection lawsuit has been filed against your or a judgment has been entered in a court of law. A court judgment allows the creditor to garnish your wages, freeze your bank accounts and even put a lien on your home. Filing for bankruptcy will stop the creditor from taking the judgment in a lawsuit or stop them from collecting if they have already done so. This is where bankruptcy will help you protect your assets including your home, your car and your wages.

A third situation arises where you have already tried to negotiate your bills but have been unsuccessful in doing so. In this situation, you have attempted to negotiate or work out a repayment plan with one or more of the companies you owe, but they will not agree to a reasonable payment or have even refused to work with you. The lender wants full payment now and aren't willing to be paid out over time. This can leave you with few options other than to file for bankruptcy.

Another common situation people find themselves in that may require personal bankruptcy is when they are behind on their home or car payments and are seeking to prevent repossession or foreclosure. A bankruptcy repayment plan will get you caught up on the payments you have missed. This type of case prevents repossession of your car. It also stops a foreclosure lawsuit immediately and will keep you and your family in your home.

Finally, filing for bankruptcy will stop the harassment. Creditor harassment through letters and especially repeated

Celebrity Bankruptcy Spotlight

Burt Reynolds, actor: Filed for Chapter 11 in 1996 after a restaurant failure and an expensive divorce.

phone calls will stop the moment you file your case. This alone is an emotional lift for most people. Creditors call at home, on the cell phone and even at work! The constant harassment is a source of stress and embarrassment that will be forever gone from your life.

3. Determine if You Even Qualify to File

Under the new bankruptcy laws enacted in 2005, not everyone will qualify for bankruptcy and even those who do may only qualify for certain kinds of relief. To determine if you qualify for bankruptcy and what type of case will work best for you, numerous factors must be considered. Successful filing for bankruptcy will be based, among other things, on the type of assets you hold, the amount of income you make and the problems you are seeking to solve.

The types of bankruptcy are Chapter 7, Chapter 11, and Chapter 13. They will be explained in more detail in the next chapter.

You must be under a certain level of income in order to qualify for Chapter 7 bankruptcy. That amount is determined by your household size and the geographical region in which you live . The next qualification for Chapter 7 bankruptcy is the assets you hold. Generally, you will not want to file for Chapter

7 if you are in title to any assets that could be sold for a profit above and beyond your state's exemptions and the excess money paid to your creditors. , you would not want to file Chapter 7 if the type of debts you have cannot be Discharge (eliminated) by the filing of the case. You will also not qualify if you have been Discharge in a previous Chapter 7 case within the last eight years.

Generally most everyone qualifies for a Chapter 13 bankruptcy provided they have regular and ongoing monthly income. A Chapter 13 case may not be a good fit if you have filed previous Chapter 7 case within the last four years or a Chapter 13 case within the last two. Additionally, if you have had one or more Chapter 13 cases dismissed within the twelve months prior to the filing of a new Chapter 13 case, you will have to have a hearing asking a judge for permission to be in the new Chapter 13 case. You will have to show that the new case was filed in "good faith." Finally, it is important to note that Chapter 13 has debt limits for both secured and unsecured debt. If you exceed those limits you may not qualify for relief in a Chapter 13 case.

The 2005 changes to the bankruptcy laws make this a complicated proposition. An experienced bankruptcy lawyer can assess these factors, give you your options and make a recommendation as to what course of action you should take. Most, if not all, bankruptcy lawyers offer this advice for free in the form of an initial consultation. The free consultation is a great way for you to find out what your options are and if bankruptcy is right for you. It is also an opportunity for you to get to know your lawyer and for him or her to get to know you. Having a good relationship with your attorney (and office staff) is arguably the most important aspect of hiring someone to help you solve your problems. You are taking the first step on the path to your future. Getting the case done right the first time is far more important than cutting costs. Find an attorney and law firm you are comfortable with and believe you could have a relationship with now and for future legal problems as they arise.

Celebrity Bankruptcy Spotlight

Tom Petty, singer: Despite early success with his band, the Heartbreakers, Tom Petty did not get rich quickly due to a restrictive recording contract. He filed for bankruptcy in 1979 after shelling out $500,000 of his own money to record an album.

Chapter Three: Bankruptcy Myths

There are many myths surrounding filing for bankruptcy and what you can and cannot do. The following paragraphs outline some of the more common myths about personal bankruptcy along with the actual truth about those myths. As you read through these myths, you will notice that all of them are far from the truth and, in most cases, the direct opposite of what really happens when you choose to exercise your rights under bankruptcy law.

Myth: ***Bankruptcy permanently ruins your credit OR you cannot get credit after bankruptcy.***

Truth: This myth is the most common misconception about bankruptcy! In general, people who file bankruptcy are often surprised by how quickly they can build credit after filing for bankruptcy. Often times they will start getting credit card offers in the mail, sometimes even within a month of the Discharge. This is due to credit scoring.

Your credit score is determined from many factors, but the two most important are a credit history and outstanding debt. Filing for bankruptcy will have a negative impact on the credit history portion of your credit score. However, when you file for bankruptcy, most (if not all) of you consumer debt is eliminated. This will give you a very positive effect in the outstanding debt category and can even raise your credit score. Bankruptcy will not prevent you from getting a really good score (even above 700) in less than two years after Discharge.

Bankruptcy generally will not prevent you from getting a good rate on a car loan or personal loan as well. More importantly, most filers find that with the proper down payment and employment history, they will become eligible for a home loan within two years after completion of the case. Our clients tell often tell us how easily they got credit after bankruptcy and how quickly their credit score recovered.

This myth persists only because people hear or read about bankruptcy affecting them for "ten years." Many people think that having a bankruptcy listed on your credit report automatically means that your credit will be bad or even ruined. People will often assume that if bankruptcy is listed on your credit report, you will not be able to buy a car, buy a house or get another loan. This is totally wrong.

It is true that bankruptcy can stay listed on your credit report for up to ten years. That is where the idea of ten years comes from. However, credit reports generally value information listed on a weighted average. This means that the newer something is, the more effect it will have on your score. Thus, after some time the fact that you filed for bankruptcy will be almost meaningless to your credit score.

Myth: ***Bankruptcy represents failure OR people who file for bankruptcy are financially irresponsible.***

Truth: Nobody files for bankruptcy because they want to, they do it because they have to. Bankruptcy is almost always caused by factors out of the control of the person who files. In fact, most every personal bankruptcy case can be tied to one of three reasons: Illness, Loss of Job and Divorce. These are factors that are beyond our control yet directly contribute to deep financial distress. Year after year the majority of people who choose to file for bankruptcy can tie the contributing or underlying factors to one or more of these three reasons.

Long-term unemployment can be devastating on your financial health and that of your family. No one chooses to be unemployed. Loss of steady income means not only having to not pay your debts but also struggling just to get by. Due to the recession that began in 2008, millions of Americans have been unemployed for six months or longer (according to the Bureau of Labor Statistics). When unemployment occurs, most people rightly focus on their day-to-day needs first and think about past due bills thereafter. This can cause the bills to increase beyond what you can ever hope to repay – even if you get a new job.

Divorce is also something that is out of the control of most people. Very few people purposefully end something they have spent so much time and effort to build. Unfortunately, it often needs to happen for the mental health of the parties involved. When divorce occurs, income is split and expenses are doubled. The legal fees associated with divorce and the cost of running two households following a divorce will often force both parties into bankruptcy through no fault of their own.

Finally, illness and the resulting medical bills are also a factor beyond our control that can force filing for bankruptcy. The high cost of medical care has driven many well-intentioned people into bankruptcy.

Bankruptcy is not a reflection of the character or integrity of the person who files. Rather, it is an option available under federal law for individuals and families to obtain much needed relief. Whatever the causes and reasons for filing, most people are not in bankruptcy because they didn't 'work hard' but because of factors beyond their control. People are in bankruptcy because, despite their best efforts, life became more than any one person could be expected to handle on their own.

Myth: ***Bankruptcy discharges (eliminates) ALL past debts.***

Truth: Many people file bankruptcy hoping they'll be able to start fresh afterwards, but several types of debt are not discharged by bankruptcy, including but not limited to student loans, money loaned for an educational benefit, certain tax debts, fines owed to governmental units, parking tickets, debts incurred by fraudulent means, including but not limited to recent cash advances or usage or recent loans, debts incurred as a result of driving under the influence of alcohol or drugs, domestic support obligations including child support and alimony and intentional torts.

Celebrity Bankruptcy Spotlight

Dionne Warwick, singer: Dionne Warwick filed for personal bankruptcy in 2013 after accruing debts of $10 million in unpaid taxes.

Myth: ***If you run up your credit cards or incur loans right before bankruptcy, you won't have to pay that money back.***

Truth: Most, if not all, courts have rulings that intentional use of credit just prior to bankruptcy filing known you will never pay it back is considered fraud, and debt from fraud is not dischargeable in a bankruptcy case. Once you know you are going to file, you should not use any more of your existing credit but, in many cases, you can stop paying on the debt that will be included and discharged.

Myth: ***Bankruptcy is a cure-all OR bankruptcy fixes all problems in your financial life.***

Truth: Chapter 7 bankruptcy discharges certain debts, while Chapter 13 may reduce or reorganize debts. However, neither one offers an easy solution. Many people think that a bankruptcy case will solve all their problems, and it may not. This is why it is important to have an experienced attorney handle your case. In Chapter 7, you may lose non-exempt assets or run into non-dischargeable debt. In Chapter 13, you could keep your house or car but also have a three to five year payment plan. It can be difficult to keep making payments as your financial situation. Chapter 13 may require you to have a very modest lifestyle if you are to complete the plan.

Myth: ***If you have been sued by a creditor, it is too late to file for bankruptcy.***

Truth: This is absolutely untrue. Bankruptcy will immediately stop any pending action, including lawsuits, foreclosure and the judicial or sheriff sale of a home. In fact, it is the best tool to keep you from losing your home. Additionally, filing for bankruptcy can prevent a levy and stop wage garnishment. In some cases it can force the return of repossessed property, like a car.

Bankruptcy protections are legally termed The Automatic Stay and they arise under section 362 of the Bankruptcy Code. The Automatic Stay is a very powerful provision of law and it forces all creditors to cease collection activities immediately.

Myth: ***It is more difficult to file bankruptcy after the 2005 law changes.***

Truth: While the 2005 law changed bankruptcy forever, it did not have the consequences that banks and other money lenders intended. (See Chapter Seven of this book for more detailed information on those changes). Although the new bankruptcy law *operates* in different manner than prior to the changes, many of the *results* are the same as they were before the law changed in 2005.

Just as many people file now as before the law changed, and those who do still receive their Discharge of debt in bankruptcy.

The new bankruptcy law was drafted primarily to prevent fraud and the changes instituted were geared toward preventing this kind of abuse. Because the vast majority of people who file for bankruptcy have not committed fraud, the results then remained the same. The new law was also drafted to determine the type of case filing by household income level. Those income levels are based on IRS guidelines. As it turns out, the guidelines are extremely accurate and affect very few people who file. Most of the people who file get the same chapter of bankruptcy and type of relief they would have before the 2005 changes.

What all this means is that the relief that was available before the 2005 changes to the law is still available now. The reasons people file a bankruptcy case did not change just because the law changed. It is true that the rumors about around the 2005 law changes still persist more than ten years later. This is why it is so important that you get accurate information about what the bankruptcy laws can do for you before you make any decisions.

The 2005 law changes made bankruptcy a bit harder to complete, but they did not change the results that you can achieve from filing.

Myth: ***You should cash in your 401K or retirement plan before filing for bankruptcy.***

Truth: Retirement funds are "exempt" or fully protected from seizure by the court in bankruptcy. There is no limit to this exemption. This means there is no limit to the amount of money you can have in the qualified retirement account and retain the funds.

The money must remain within the retirement account, however. If you decide to draw upon your retirement funds prematurely to pay creditors, it could have very serious income tax implications and penalties must be paid on the withdraw. By taking the money, you may have to turn these exempt funds into assets that a bankruptcy court can liquidate to pay your creditors.

Myth: ***You can't afford to talk to an attorney.***

Truth: This is also untrue. Almost every bankruptcy attorney or bankruptcy law firm offers a free initial consultation. This is a great way for you to see if you have a case and what chapter of bankruptcy you should file. It will not only give you an opportunity to meet the lawyer and law firm before you hire them, but for them to meet you. In this way you can determine if the firm and its attorneys and staff are a good fit for you. Every single client who has come to see me over the almost twenty years I have been practicing consumer bankruptcy law has been shown, for free, what their options and rights are under the law and then quoted an exact price for me and my firm to do the work – before ever committing to pay anything.

Sometimes the biggest obstacle to making bankruptcy work is just scheduling the free consultation with our office, where we can speak to you one-on-one about your financial situation, as well as provide information regarding legal fees and tailored payment options.

Myth: ***If you can't afford to pay creditors, you can't afford to pay an attorney.***

Truth: My firm offers a flexible payment plan for just about everyone who wants to file a case, including those on a fixed

Celebrity Bankruptcy Spotlight

Wayne Newton, entertainer: Despite once being listed as the highest paid entertainer in the world, Wayne Newton eventually amassed enormous debt and filed for Chapter 11 bankruptcy in the early 1990s.

income. In fact, most bankruptcy law firms do this. It goes hand in hand with the nature of bankruptcy. I have worked with thousands of individuals and families in the past and have done everything possible to create a flexible environment to help our clients manage their legal fees and to meet their unique needs.

Many times, people will try to obtain legal advice from the internet, co-workers, family or friends. In my experience, this is one of the worst things a person can do. The information is not always accurate and is often misleading. This misinformation tends to make the situation more difficult emotionally and even financially if you choose costly non-bankruptcy alternatives before talking to a lawyer. You can get the facts and take the fear out of bankruptcy with a free consultation from our firm. Your situation is always private, protected by attorney-client privilege and the solution will be personalized to your unique financial situation.

Myth: ***When married, the bankruptcy filing of one spouse will ruin the credit of the other.***

Truth: The Bankruptcy Code permits an individual spouse to file bankruptcy without the need for the other spouse to "join in" on the filing. Not only can the spouse who files eliminate individual debt, but the other spouse's credit should not be affected in any way.

The key to filing individually and not as a married couple is that only the individual debt of the spouse who files will be eliminated. Joint debt will remain the responsibility of the non-filing spouse. Joint credit cards can create problems in this scenario. This is why you will want an experienced attorney to thoroughly review your specific situation. I will always show a married couple what the results will be if both or only one of them files. Along the same lines, a bankruptcy filing by an individual before marriage will not affect the credit of a new spouse.

Myth: ***You must be behind on your bills to file for bankruptcy.***

Truth: There is no legal requirement that you be behind in payments in order to file for bankruptcy. However, even if you are making the minimum payment on your bills, you are not solving your problems. In some cases, credit card and other minimum payment plans are calculated so that you will almost never be able to pay them off. Paying minimum payments is only a short term solution that does not solve the real problem. The problem is that by the time you realize you are in the cycle of minimum payments, it is too late to recover. Most of my clients have struggled for many years before they sought the advice of an attorney.

Myth: ***There is a debt "minimum" necessary to file for bankruptcy.***

Truth: There is NO debt "minimum" necessary to file for bankruptcy. You could file bankruptcy on a one dollar debt if you wished, but it would not make financial sense to do so. I often tell my clients that they need to look at their total debt versus how much the bankruptcy will cost. In most cases, the legal fee amounts to a very small percentage of the total debt eliminated, so it almost always a great deal. With that said, it is worthwhile to mention that even a small amount of debt can become a problem if neglected.

Myth: ***You can lose your job due to bankruptcy.***

Truth: Pursuant to Federal law (11 U.S.C. Sec. 525) any employer is forbidden from discriminating against you because you filed bankruptcy.

This is a very common question, asked by almost every client I meet with. However, it rarely (if ever!) comes up in life after bankruptcy. I have represented thousands of people and have never once seen someone fired for a bankruptcy filing. The only industry that seems to dislike bankruptcy on a job application is the banking industry, but it is still bound by federal law 11 U.S.C. Sec. 525. The reason the banking industry does not like bankruptcy filing is because it eliminates debt they are owed – not because you are working with money. In reality, an employee that has filed for bankruptcy has much less temptation to misappropriate funds as they have already eliminated their personal financial problems by filing bankruptcy and have no need for the money.

Myth: ***If you filed bankruptcy before, you cannot file again.***

Truth: In some instances, the bankruptcy law will permit a new discharge in as little as four years. Changes made to the bankruptcy law in 2005 created a scenario where debtors can seek Chapter 7 relief once every eight years. However, debtors can seek Chapter 13 relief in only four years following a Chapter 7 bankruptcy, if necessary.

Myth: ***Creditors can continue to harass you after bankruptcy.***

Truth: Once bankruptcy is filed, creditors are NOT permitted to contact you for any reason, including but not limited to collection actions. Bankruptcy Code Section 362 has a broad definition of collection action, so that means almost anything anyone you owe money to does to you after the filing is illegal. The Bankruptcy Code is also very specific as to creditor harassment in bankruptcy. Phone calls, mail, email, repossession actions, utility shut-offs, foreclosure, lawsuits and any other type of harassment must stop when the case is filed.

Myth: ***Medical bills cannot be discharged in bankruptcy.***

Truth: Untrue. Even under the new healthcare laws, medical bills, credit card bills and personal loans can be discharged in bankruptcy. This myth is extremely common and couldn't be farther from the truth. The Federal Bankruptcy Code does not give special treatment in bankruptcy for medical bills. Medical bills can be eliminated in bankruptcy.

Myth: ***My bankruptcy will show up online and in the newspaper and "everyone" will know.***

Truth: In most, if not all cases, someone will only find out you filed for bankruptcy if you tell them. That is because while filing is

Celebrity Bankruptcy Spotlight

Mark Twain, writer: Samuel Clemens was deep in debt due to a few bad investments. After getting rid of his publishing house and assigning copyrights to his wife, he declared bankruptcy in 1894.

a matter of public record (like a divorce filing), the information is not actively sent out to the general public. If someone wants to find out if you have filed for bankruptcy, they will have to specifically search out that information.

Myth: ***You will lose everything you own when you file for bankruptcy.***

Truth: In almost all cases the answer is "no." You can keep your home, cars, household goods and pension. The Bankruptcy laws provide specific "exemptions" or protections for most basic possessions. In general, proper exemption planning will allow you to retain your basic assets to so that you can get a true fresh start. In a Chapter 13 bankruptcy, none of your property is claimed by the court or creditors. In a Chapter 7 bankruptcy, things that are non-exempt may be claimed by creditors for liquidation. Exemptions are determined by state law, and we can discuss what exemptions may apply to you during a consultation.

Myth: ***Debt consolidation companies are better than bankruptcy.***

Truth: Many of the programs offered by debt consolidation companies just make the problem worse and ultimately end in failure. In some cases they are even scams that can ruin your credit. Not all debt consolidation companies are bad, but there are so many that are not legitimate that it is hard to know the good ones from bad.

Also, unlike federal bankruptcy law, there is very minimal regulation of these companies. Generally by the time someone comes to our firm after using a debt consolidator, they are further in debt than when they started. This is because the debt consolidators do not eliminate debt under law or even pay it off. They simply try to negotiate a payment plan – which is extremely difficult to do with little money to offer. It is important to remember the unlike debt consolidation companies, bankruptcy attorneys are regulated by state law and by the federal bankruptcy laws.

Where Do the Bankruptcy Myths and Lies Come From?

There are more myths about bankruptcy than can be listed here. Most of the myths and misinformation come from one of several sources:

First, they come from other people with good intentions who don't know or understand the facts about bankruptcy. It is like a rumor mill that just keeps feeding itself. The bad information might even come from friends or trusted family members who just have it wrong. It is important to remember not to blame them. It is generally not the fault of that person. Hundreds of millions of dollars are spent on bankruptcy propaganda every year trying to put out false information. Even good, smart people can fall victim to these types of campaigns.

A second source of misinformation is from the debt negotiation and debt consolidation industry. As mentioned previously, there are many less than reputable companies that mislead people. The debt consolidation and negotiation industry is far larger than bankruptcy and generates a lot more money. These companies have a financial incentive to scare you away from bankruptcy, which is a far more effective and lower cost alternative.

The third major source is the credit card companies that want to scare you away because they want you to keep paying interest.

Finally, there are the financial journalists and economic advisors in the general medial. The information they put out is often done to generate headlines with little research behind it. Some may even want to build a fan base by saying controversial things. Others are just repeating what they have heard much like an uniformed friend or family member. In either case it continues in keeping these myths alive.

It is important to remember that these myths are just that—myths. Bankruptcy is a federal law. And like every other federal law, it is designed for your protection.

Chapter Four: Which Type of Bankruptcy is Right for Me?

As touched on previously, determining which type of bankruptcy case is right for you is best done by an experienced bankruptcy attorney. So many factors go into making the determination that this is where experience and a deep understanding of the process are critical. The initial consultation with a bankruptcy lawyer is almost always free, and I recommend you take advantage of this fact when getting started.

In this section, I have included a description of each type of bankruptcy that an individual (consumer) may file and when that type of case is generally appropriate. Remember, these descriptions of the types of bankruptcy are for informational purposes only and are intended to give you an understanding of the types of bankruptcy cases—not a specific recommendation as to which one you should file. I am hopeful that you will use what you learn here when you meet with an attorney so that you can make an informed choice when he or she gives you your options under bankruptcy law.

Chapter 7 Bankruptcy

This is the most common and widely used form of bankruptcy for individuals. It is probably the type of case that you think of when you hear the word "bankruptcy." In general, Chapter 7 Bankruptcy eliminates your debt. What this means is that you will no longer be legally liable for the debt once you file and complete the case. This type of case is good for getting rid of "unsecured" debts. Unsecured debts are those debts which are not secured in property, sometimes known as collateral. With an unsecured debt, the person you owe has no right in anything you own—there is no collateral. Common unsecured debts are credit cards, personal loans, "payday" loans, personal lines of credit, old cell phone bills, cable bills and, of course, medical bills. All of these types of debt, as well as many others, will be wiped out by the successful completion of a Chapter 7 Bankruptcy case.

Celebrity Bankruptcy Spotlight

Donald Trump, real estate investor: This famously rich man has filed for bankruptcy four times—in 1991, 1992, 2004 and 2009.

A Chapter 7 Bankruptcy case, in general, will not change the security interest a lender may have where property has been pledged as a security interest (collateral). The most common of these are your home or car. In a Chapter 7 Bankruptcy, you may be able to keep your home or car but you will have to continue to make the payments to do so. The filing of the case only eliminates the need for car payments or mortgage payments if you surrender the property back to the lender. I tell my clients that the best way to think of this is that the lender or bank is holding on to you with one hand and onto the collateral with the other. The Chapter 7 Bankruptcy filing causes them to let go of you (no more personal liability for the debt, BUT they continue to hold on to the pledged collateral). In most cases, the lien of the lender survives the bankruptcy. It may be possible to remove judgment liens from a home in Chapter 7 Bankruptcy in limited circumstances.

Other types of secured liens that may survive Chapter 7 Bankruptcy are purchase money security interests and tax liens. Tax liens, of course, are those liens placed by the government for past due taxes. Purchase money security interests, however, are liens on those items financed directly by the seller. Common examples include jewelry and furniture. Be sure to let your attorney know of these types of arrangements when deciding to file Chapter 7 Bankruptcy.

An individual who files for Chapter 7 Bankruptcy must be income qualified to do so. This means that your total household income must fall below average income (as determined by IRS guidelines) for your household size and geographical location.

Chapter 13 Bankruptcy

A Chapter 13 Bankruptcy is filed by an individual to "reorganize" his or her consumer debts. A Chapter 13 plan can stop a foreclosure, repossession or even un-suspend your driver's license. It can cure past due mortgage payments, remove "underwater" second mortgages or other liens, pay IRS and state taxes, car payments and even student loans. A Chapter 13 can also call for the partial payment of unsecured debt such as credit cards, medical bills, personal loans payday loans and utilities. Chapter 13 Bankruptcy may also be able to deal with parking tickets and toll-way violations.

The purpose of Chapter 13 is to allow an individual with regular monthly income to set up a plan to repay some or all of their debts. This is why it is sometimes referred to as a "Wage Earner's Plan," although many types of monthly income can be used to fund the plan. In addition to income from employment, a person filing Chapter 13 may also be able to base their plan on retirement income, social security/disability income, contributions from family members and in some cases unemployment income. Chapter 13 is different from debt consolidation or setting up a plan directly with the lender because you only pay back what you can afford and the rest is eliminated upon completion of the payment plan. There is also no interest on your debts in a Chapter 13 plan. In other types of plans you almost always pay the debt in full plus some form of interest.

Filers propose a Chapter 13 plan for three to five years depending on the type of debts they have and the amount of income earned by their household. Household income is the total amount of income earned by the members of your home, regardless of who is filing the case. While this may seem unfair (it is), the income of non-filing household members can be offset by their own individual expenses and debt payments. For example, if a non-filing spouse has his or her own auto loan and credit cards, they would be deducted from the total household income.

Once a case is filed and a plan proposed, you will be assigned a Chapter 13 trustee and given a meeting date with their office to discuss your Plan. The Bankruptcy Court uses a trustee to handle, track and distribute payments under the plan. At your meeting, the trustee will review your income to make sure you are able to afford the plan as proposed. He or she may suggest changes to be made to the plan in order to get it ready to go to the bankruptcy judge for approval. The people you owe money to (creditors) have a chance to object to your plan but you are given an opportunity to fix or eliminate those objections when the case goes before a Judge.

The Chapter 13 Plan continues to protect the individual filer as long as the required payments are made over the three to five years of the plan. Like a Chapter 7, the filer receives a discharge of his or her debts at the end of the plan.

Throughout the Chapter 13 Plan, it is the responsibility of the debtor (the person filing the case) to make the required payments to the trustee and to those creditors that are being paid directly and outside the plan payments. If the required payments cannot be made, you should notify your attorney as soon as possible.

It is also the debtor's responsibility to attend their meeting with the trustee, commonly called the "341 Meeting" or "Meeting of Creditors." You must be on time for the meeting and bring proof of income, a picture ID and your social security card. Failure to appear at this meeting with the proper identification may result in the dismissal of the case.

Another good practice as a debtor in Chapter 13 is to notify your attorney of any change in your personal situation throughout the three to five years you are under the plan. This includes any change in address, telephone number or email. You should also contact your attorney immediately if you lose employment, have a significant change in income/expenses or experience any other major change in your financial situation. Some of these major changes may include illness, marriage, divorce, separation, lottery winnings, or even an inheritance. It is also extremely important to notify your attorney if you are sued or wishes to file a lawsuit. This is especially true of a personal injury case (lawsuit for bodily injury such as a car accident or slip-and-fall) as a failure to inform the Bankruptcy Court may cause you to lose both the bankruptcy and the personal injury case.

You should also be sure to speak with your attorney before buying, refinancing, or selling your property and before entering into any type loan agreements.

Finally, you should keep your attorney informed as to the status of your tax filings. Some Chapter 13 Plans require a debtor to surrender their tax return to the Chapter 13 trustee to be paid

Celebrity Bankruptcy Spotlight

Toni Braxton, recording artist: This famous singer has filed for personal bankruptcy twice, once in 2010 and again in 2013.

out under their Plan. It is important that your attorney be kept informed as to your tax status. You should supply your lawyer with copies of all tax returns filed while your case is pending.

Your bankruptcy attorney will also have responsibilities and duties to you while your case is pending. The Bankruptcy Court has been clear in outlining those duties and enforcing penalties against those attorneys who fail to adequately represent their clients. The following list of an attorney's duties in a Chapter 13 Bankruptcy case is an excerpt from the Model Retention Agreement for the Northern District of Illinois (Chicago) and are some of the major items most courts will require of attorneys who represent debtors. The actual agreement may be found on that court's website at www.ilnb.uscourts.gov/forms/all-forms. The duties include:

1. Advise the debtor of the requirement to attend the meeting of creditors, and notify the debtor of the date, time, and place of the meeting.

2. Inform the debtor that the debtor must be punctual and, in the case of a joint filing, that both spouses must appear at the same meeting.

3. Provide knowledgeable legal representation for the debtor at the meeting of creditors (in time for check-in and the

actual examination) and, unless excused by the trustee, for the confirmation hearing.

4. If the attorney will be employing another attorney to attend the 341 meeting or any court hearing, personally explain to the debtor in advance, the role and identity of the other attorney and provide the other attorney with the file in sufficient time to review it and properly represent the debtor.

5. Timely submit to the Chapter 13 trustee properly documented proof of income for the debtor, including business reports for self-employed debtors.

6. Timely respond to objections to plan confirmation and, where necessary, prepare, file, and serve an amended plan.

7. Timely prepare, file, and serve any necessary statements, amended statements, and schedules and any change of address, in accordance with information provided by the debtor.

8. Monitor all incoming case information (including, but not limited to, Order Confirming Plan, Notice of Intent to Pay Claims, and 6-month status reports) for accuracy and completeness. Contact the trustee promptly regarding any discrepancies.

9. Be available to respond to the debtor's questions throughout the term of the plan.

10. Prepare, file, and serve timely modifications to the plan after confirmation, when necessary, including modifications to suspend, lower, or increase plan payments.

11. Prepare, file, and serve necessary motions to buy or sell property and to incur debt.

12. Object to improper or invalid claims.

13. Timely respond to the Chapter 13 trustee's motions to dismiss the case, such as for payment default, or unfeasibility, and to motions to increase the percentage payment to unsecured creditors.

14. Timely respond to motions for relief from stay.

15. Prepare, file, and serve all appropriate motions to avoid liens.

16. Provide any other legal services necessary for the administration of the case.

As you can see from the list above, the duties and responsibilities of a lawyer in a Chapter 13 bankruptcy are extensive and the courts have taken great pains to ensure that those attorneys who file Chapter 13 case remain involved throughout the entirety of the case.

Even with these strict regulations, many attorneys fail to properly ensure the success of their clients' cases and to be "present" in the case throughout its three to five year duration. It is therefore crucial that you choose an attorney with not only experience, but integrity as well.

In most, if not all, Chapter 13 cases, the attorney earns a flat fee for the work he or she does and that flat fee is set by the court. Usually the only difference between the fees different attorneys will charge in Chapter 13 is the amount of the money they take up front and the remainder to be paid in the plan. Thus, a Chapter 13 attorney should not be hired on price (as the total fee is usually set by the court) but on his or her ability to get the job done right repeatedly over the three to five years of the plan.

Finally, it is important to note that debt in a Chapter 13 Bankruptcy is Discharged upon completion of the plan payments. The Discharge is similar to that of a Chapter 7 case but generally includes only those debts incurred prior to the filing of the case itself.

Chapter 11 Bankruptcy

A Chapter 11 Bankruptcy is generally used by a corporation to reorganize or repay its debts. It can also be used by individuals who do not qualify for Chapter 13 Bankruptcy due to high levels of income or debt that exceed the allowed limits of Chapter 13. Chapter 11 bankruptcies are very expensive due to the large amount of attorney (and other professional) time that must be expended in order to properly prosecute the case. In fact, the cost is so much greater than consumer bankruptcies under Chapter 7 or Chapter 13 that it is often times not feasible to file the case. Chapter 11 is generally more appropriate for large enterprises seeking to reorganize the company for continued operations in the future. Two good examples of companies that successfully filed for Chapter 11 are United Airlines and the Kmart Corporation. These large companies have the financial ability to pay the legal fees necessary to reorganize under Chapter 11. Small businesses and individuals should seek other forms of relief and pursue a Chapter 11 only as a last resort.

Celebrity Bankruptcy Spotlight

Debbie Reynolds, actress: Filed for bankruptcy in 1997 after being unable to sell property in Las Vegas.

Chapter Five: The Small Business and Bankruptcy

Many people who come to see me are self-employed or the owners of a small business who are struggling with debt and wish to explore their options. There are a few different types of business bankruptcies that may be appropriate for someone with a small business, but the one that works will depend upon the nature of your business and how the debts of the business are held.

The first big question is what type of business entity do you have: sole proprietorship, corporation or limited liability company (LLC)? If you are a sole proprietor (not formally incorporated) then the debts of the business will be your debts and you must file Chapter 7 or Chapter 13, depending on what works for you personally. The analysis in this situation will be the same as filing for personal bankruptcy as I have outlined earlier in the book.

If your business is formally incorporated as a Corporation or an LLC, then I next look at the type of debts owed. Businesses have all types of debt including leases, state and federal tax obligations, secured or collateralized debts on loans to banks or other financial institutions and even money owed to vendors and suppliers. The key analysis here is if any of the debt is secured (collateralized) or personally guaranteed by the business owner. While vendors and suppliers generally do not take personal guarantees, business leases and bank loans almost always do. Banks may go so far as to take a "wrap-around" lien on all the business assets in addition to requiring a personal guarantee. You may also have personal liability for the employer portion of your state and federal employment taxes as well as any sales and use taxes from the state you live in. With these types of debts, it may be necessary to file for both the business and yourself personally.

Finally, it is important to look at the future prospects of the business. If the business is having trouble generating new customers and new income, then liquidating the business through Chapter 7 is the best option. Many small business owners will continue to run a business that is not profitable because they do not know what else to do and feel stuck in a cycle they cannot escape. This occurs when the business is generating enough revenue to keep the doors open but not enough to make money for its owners. While it can be hard to let the business go, filing Chapter 7 allows the small business owner the freedom to start a new business without all the debt obligations—even in the same or related industry!

Reorganizing a business with Chapter 11 is an expensive process and should only be done with there is a certainty that revenue will continue to come into the company and the reduction of debt will allow it to be profitable again. Undertaking a Chapter 11 Reorganization plan is something that should only be done after a thorough investigation of all aspects of the business to determine if it can be a viable entity on an ongoing basis.

Filing a bankruptcy for your business depends on many factors: whether you want to close your business or keep it running, and what type of business you have and how much and what types of debts there are. This is an area of bankruptcy where a knowledgeable and experienced attorney is not only important but vital to your success.

Celebrity Bankruptcy Spotlight

Meat Loaf, singer: After a lawsuit was brought against him in the mid 1980s, Meat Loaf declared bankruptcy.

Chapter Six: A Very Short History of Bankruptcy Laws

The United States Constitution was ratified in 1788 and it gave Congress the right to legislate "uniform laws on the subject of bankruptcies." The first bankruptcy law was the Bankruptcy Act of 1800 which was very limited and offered no voluntary protection to individuals. It only allowed for involuntary bankruptcy (persons or companies were "forced" into it by their Creditors). It did not last long and was repealed in 1803. Voluntary bankruptcy was first allowed in the Bankruptcy Act of 1841. It was expanded in 1867 and again with the Nelson Act in 1898. These Acts established the concepts of modern day bankruptcy law and the relationship between lenders and borrowers in bankruptcy.

The next century saw the enactment of The Bankruptcy Act of 1938. This law was known as the Chandler Act and it allowed greater access to bankruptcy for those seeking voluntary protection without being forced into bankruptcy. The next major (and very important) change came with the Bankruptcy Reform Act of 1978. The Reform Act was a major overhaul of the entire bankruptcy system. While the changes in the law were significant, the most important change by the Reform Act was the broad expansion of the Bankruptcy Courts and their jurisdiction. This part of the law was declared unconstitutional and the Bankruptcy Amendments of 1984 were enacted to fix the problem and secure the jurisdiction of Bankruptcy judges and courts. In 1994, the Bankruptcy Reform Act was signed into law to deal with the problems created by the intersection of bankruptcy and the mortgage banking industry.

Perhaps the most significant change in the bankruptcy laws since their inception in 1800 is the Bankruptcy Abuse Prevention and Consumer Protection Act of 2005. This is the law that is still in place today and its enactment significantly changed how individuals file for bankruptcy. I cover the details in the next chapter.

Celebrity Bankruptcy Spotlight

Janice Dickinson, model: In April of 2013, the former model filed for bankruptcy over a reported $1 million in debt.

Chapter Seven: 2005: Personal Bankruptcy Changes Forever

On October 17, 2005, the new consumer bankruptcy laws went into effect and forever changed how personal bankruptcy works in the United States. Prior to that date, filing personal bankruptcy was primarily dependent on the assets you had in your possession. This meant that virtually everyone could file a Chapter 7 Bankruptcy and eliminate their debts. The only risk would be the sale of assets owned. The new bankruptcy law (called the Bankruptcy Abuse and Consumer Protection Act) now added a new dimension to qualifying for bankruptcy protection: household income. People earning more than a certain amount would now have to pay at least some of their debt back.

Prior to the 2005 changes in the law, people of all income levels could file for Chapter 7 Bankruptcy. By instituting an income test, the new law sought to limit those who could file for Chapter 7. The income test is based on IRS standards for the median (average) income for differing household sizes. The IRS standards are set out for each county and each state. If your total household income is below the IRS average for the state and county you live in, you generally qualify for Chapter 7. If it is above the IRS average, then you are evaluated by a complex mathematical formula to see if you qualify for Chapter 7 or how much you will have to pay monthly in a Chapter 13 Bankruptcy repayment plan. This extremely complicated formula is known as the Means Test.

The Means Test calculates your current monthly income and compares it to your current monthly expenses to determine how much (if any) debt you will have to repay. The test calculates these figures by averaging the previous six months of your household income from all sources. Almost all sources of income are considered, including but not limited to your job, any part time employment, rents received, gift income, retirement or pension income, self-employment and even unemployment. Social security payments are not included in the calculation along with a few other exceptions. If you are married and your spouse is not filing the bankruptcy as well, you will still have to submit their income information to assist in the calculation of total household income. You may be able to subtract out all or part of your spouse's income depending on his or her monthly debt obligations.

Once your total income is calculated, the formula then compares it to a set of expenses. Those expenses are based on IRS guidelines as well as local court standards. Some of the expenses and deductions include mortgage or rent payments, real estate taxes, utilities, car payments, home and auto insurance, health insurance, life insurance, disability insurance, medical spending, health savings accounts, schooling expenses, charitable contributions and income taxes. There are other deductions and expenses that apply in certain circumstances as well.

A good bankruptcy attorney is vital when going through Means Testing. The Means Test can make or break your bankruptcy case. It will determine if you can file Chapter 7 and get rid of all your debt; or if you have to repay, it will determine your monthly payments. A good attorney will be able to maximize your position under the Means Test and get rid of the greatest amount of debt for you.

The Means Test is related to the concept of "Abuse" as laid out in the new bankruptcy law. The law presumes that abuse of the law arises when you have money left over after the Means Test calculation. This means that the law just assumes you can repay much more of your debts—no matter your circumstances! Another reason a good attorney is so important.

Celebrity Bankruptcy Spotlight

Mickey Rooney, actor: When Mickey Rooney filed for bankruptcy in 1962, his personal assets were listed at $500.

In addition to adding an income test, the new bankruptcy laws of 2005 also instituted many other changes. One of those changes was the requirement that any individual seeking bankruptcy protection has to take a Counseling Course prior to the filing of the case. Failure to take the course prior to filing a case will result in dismissal of the case. When you take the course, the certificate of completion is only good for one hundred eighty days. If you do not file your bankruptcy case within that time, you will be required to take (and pay) for the course all over again. In addition to the pre-filing course, a second course, called Debtor Education, must be taken prior to completion of the case. If your case is closed without taking this exit-counseling course, the court will not allow successful completion of the case and elimination of your debts going forward. These two courses create a hurdle that must now be cleared in order to successfully file and complete your bankruptcy case.

Another paperwork hurdle that was added by the new bankruptcy law is the requirement to provide financial documentation to the bankruptcy trustee. Prior to the 2005 amendments, a bankruptcy filer's signature validated the information in their case. Now, individuals must provide several years of federal tax returns, income information (including but not limited to paycheck stubs, unemployment statements, social security and disability payments, rents) and even bank statements if requested. While this information is designed to support the calculations of the Means Test and the information contained in the bankruptcy schedules, it may be difficult to obtain and can also present a misleading picture to the court. This occurs when your income and expenses have changed (job shift, housing switch, etc.) making the information from past six months not relevant to your budget and ability to pay on a going forward basis. It can be difficult to convince the court and bankruptcy trustees of your change in situation, and this can ultimately impact the type and extent of relief you can obtain.

An additional change coming out of the 2005 law revisions was the increased waiting time between case filings. Previously, an individual had to wait six years between filing Chapter 7 bankruptcies. The new law increased that waiting period to eight years. This was a major setback as a financial hardship can happen at any time—not just every eight years.

Along with the waiting time increase for Chapter 7, the 2005 laws also made refiling a Chapter 13 Bankruptcy plan much harder. Previously, if your Chapter 13 case was dismissed, you could file a new case right away and automatically resume protection under the law. Now, under the new bankruptcy laws, if you re-file a Chapter 13 case within one year of the dismissal of a previous case, your bankruptcy protection will only last for thirty days. Thus, you must go to court within thirty days of the filing of the case and have a hearing on whether there is a good faith basis to allow the new case. The judge will make a determination of good faith on a case by case basis. This determination will be based on the facts and evidence presented in your request to keep the case and may even require testimony at a hearing. It is one of the more complicated aspects of the new law revisions and will almost always require an attorney.

The situation is even more difficult if you are filing a case within one year after two previous Chapter 13 cases have been dismissed. In this instance, you will get no bankruptcy protection upon the filing of your case. You must go to court and have a hearing with a judge to determine if you are entitled to any bankruptcy protection. This creates the problem that creditors can still foreclose your home, repossess vehicles, freeze bank accounts and garnish wages until the entry of the court order. They may get the things you are trying to protect before you can obtain any type of bankruptcy protection. This makes for a very difficult situation.

The new bankruptcy laws also put into place stricter noticing requirements to creditors as well. Creditors (people you owe money to) are entitled to notice of the bankruptcy filing at either an address on file with the Bankruptcy Court or at "an address stated in two communications from the creditor to the debtor within ninety days of the filing of the bankruptcy case." This means the individual filing for bankruptcy must figure out the last two letters or bills they received from a creditor, determine if it contains the same address in both and make sure bankruptcy notice is sent there. This is a very difficult "hoop" to jump through as an individual may not be able to locate the two most recent notices from the creditor. The law does allow for later cure of this problem is the creditor does receive notice by the person formally designated to receive bankruptcy notice. The Bankruptcy Court has also stepped in to assist in this issue through the creation of a database for noticing creditors when sending out their official Notice of Commencement of Case.

The new bankruptcy laws also include limits to the amount of exemptions a bankruptcy filer can use to protect his or her assets. Exemptions are laws written by each state that allow protection of property from collection or seizure by creditors. Exemption laws set out how much of each specific type of property can be protected from collection. These laws are applied in bankruptcy by prevent the liquidation (sale) of assets by the Bankruptcy Court. The major change was in the Homestead Exemption—the exemption which protects your home from creditors. The new bankruptcy law limited the ability of bankruptcy filers to move to a different state and use that state's homestead exemptions to protect their assets. Before the changes to the bankruptcy law, an individual could move to any state and enjoy its protections. The new law now requires that you live in the state for two years before you can use its exemption laws and forty months before you can protect a newly acquired home. This was done to prevent people from moving from one state to another to take advantage of that state's more favorable exemption laws.

Student loans are another area made less favorable by the 2005 changes in the bankruptcy laws. Student loans, which were already very hard to eliminate in bankruptcy, were made even more difficult to discharge under the new bankruptcy laws. The law changed to state that any money lent for an "educational purpose" could not be discharged. This means that loans from for-profit schools, not just those from traditional colleges and universities, will not be eliminated by the filing for bankruptcy.

One final major change to the law was the large increase in the court filing fee for each chapter of bankruptcy. This is significant because it set a trend for fee increases that has continued through today.

Celebrity Bankruptcy Spotlight

Larry King, radio and TV personality: Prior to being the star of his own show, Larry King filed for bankruptcy in 1978 after amassing $352,000 in debt.

Chapter Eight: Final Thoughts

I have been a bankruptcy lawyer for just about twenty years and have been involved with all aspects of filing for bankruptcy. Over the years, our firm has helped thousands of clients, each with their individual issues and problems.

Recently, we filed a case for an elderly client who was overwhelmed by harassing phone calls for debts he could never repay on his fixed income. His total debt was not exceedingly large by bankruptcy standards, but filing bankruptcy stopped the phone calls and the stress. He told me that while filing was a hard decision for him based on the way he was raised, that the harassment was so bad he was having physical and mental issues as a result. Filing his case was as much stress relief as debt relief.

In another case, our firm filed a bankruptcy for a young couple with no health insurance who had just had a baby. Complications as a result of pregnancy caused their medical bills to be very high with no way for the young couple to pay. Through bankruptcy, they were able to eliminate the debt and start their new family on a solid financial footing.

We also filed a case for the return of a vehicle belonging to a single mother who needed it to get to work to support her nine year old son.

These are just a few of the stories of the thousands of people we help year after year. Bankruptcy is one of the most powerful laws that an individual can use to protect themselves from banks and other lenders who hold all the power in a consumer transaction. Bankruptcy is a federal law designed for your protection. It reduces or eliminates your debts in order to give you a fresh start in your personal and financial life. It is a concept that at its core is really very simple.

Unfortunately, bankruptcy is also a law that is extremely misunderstood and surrounded by myths and misinformation. I wrote this book to help individuals and families get the facts about the bankruptcy laws straight from a lawyer *before* they begin the process.

I am hopeful that this book will help everyone who reads it to gain information and insight into a law that I believe has the power to change your life for the better and in some cases provide relief that is nothing short of a miracle. Our firm has story after story of clients who, after filing, come in with hugs and tears of joy at being debt free and almost all of them say that they wish they had done it sooner!

Filing for bankruptcy does not just eliminate debts and restructure your finances; it eliminates your stress and restructures your life. As you have seen with the many celebrities who have filed for bankruptcy protection, it is a game changer. It is my belief that taking action through bankruptcy can give people a true "new" beginning on life.

About the Author

Attorney Mark R. Schottler

Mr. Schottler has been practicing law since 1996 and has extensive experience in the area of commercial litigation and bankruptcy. He is a graduate of the JD/MBA program at Marquette University, earning both a law degree from the Law School and an MBA from the Graduate School of Management.

After graduating from law school, he worked as an attorney for two Chapter 7 Bankruptcy Trustees before starting his own firm, Schottler & Associates. Mr. Schottler has represented individual and corporate debtors and creditors as well as Chapter 7 bankruptcy trustees.

He is currently licensed to practice law in Illinois and Wisconsin and practices throughout the Chicagoland area.

Glossary of Personal Bankruptcy Terms

Adequate Protection – the right of a party with an interest in the debtor's property (such as a secured creditor) to assurance that its interest will not be diminished during the bankruptcy.

Administrative Claim (or **Administrative Expense Claim**) – debt incurred by the debtor, with court approval, after the bankruptcy filing including: necessary costs of preserving the estate, wages, salaries, court costs, lawyers' fees, accountants' fees, trustees' expenses, etc.

Adversary Proceeding – a lawsuit arising in or related to a bankruptcy case that is commenced by filing a complaint with the bankruptcy court.

Allowed Claim – a claim of a creditor (or an equity interest) that is approved by the court under the plan of reorganization.

Assume – an agreement to continue performing duties under a contract or lease.

Automatic Stay – the suspension of actions, such as debt collection or foreclosure, against the company in bankruptcy. This occurs automatically when a bankruptcy petition is filed. This action protects the debtor from creditors seeking to seize its assets. It protects some creditors in that it prevents one creditor from obtaining an excessive share of the assets of the bankrupt company to the exclusion of the other creditors. Section 362 of the Bankruptcy Code.

Bankruptcy – a legal procedure for dealing with debt problems of individuals and business under Federal Law. A non-technical term for a legal state of insolvency.

Bankruptcy Abuse Prevention and Consumer Protection Act (BAPCPA) of 2005 – This legislation primarily affects consumer filings, making it more difficult for a person or estate to file for Chapter 7 bankruptcy. The BAPCPA impacts business filers as well--with the heaviest impact on smaller (those listing less than $2 million in debt) businesses. On October 17, 2005 the BAPCPA became effective.

Bankruptcy Code – the name given to the statutory body of bankruptcy laws after the Bankruptcy Reform Act of 1978.

Bankruptcy Court – the federal tribunal where cases under the Bankruptcy Code are litigated.

Bankruptcy Estate – all legal or equitable interests of the debtor in property at the time of the bankruptcy filing. The estate includes all property in which the debtor has an interest, even if it is owned or held by another person.

Bankruptcy Judge – a judicial officer of the United States district court with decision-making power over federal bankruptcy cases.

Bankruptcy Petition – the document filed with the court to initiate a bankruptcy proceeding.

Bankruptcy Rule 2004 – a provision of the Bankruptcy Code that allows one party in a bankruptcy proceeding to compel discovery or other examination against another party. Debtors may be subject to a "2004 Exam" similar to a deposition.

Bar Date – the last date that creditors may file a claim against the debtor. Also called Claims Bar Date.

Business Bankruptcy – a bankruptcy case in which the debtor is a business or an individual with business related debt. Data from the U.S. Administrative Office of the Courts subdivides bankruptcies into business and non-business. Also call Corporate Bankrutpcy.

Cash Collateral – cash and cash equivalents held by the debtor in Chapter 11 subject to liens of other parties. May occur in Chapter 13 with apartment buildings and small businesses.

Chapter – the Bankruptcy Code is organized into Chapters. Except for Chapter 12, the Chapters of the present code are all odd-numbered and are enumerated with Arabic numerals. (Before the Bankruptcy Reform Act of 1978, the Chapters were numbered with Roman numerals.) Chapters 1, 3, and 5 cover matters of general application. Chapters 7, 9, 11, 12, 13 and 15 concern, respectively: liquidation (business or non-business), municipality bankruptcy; business reorganization, family farm debt adjustment, wage-earner or personal (i.e. non-business) reorganization and multi-national bankruptcies.

Chapter 7 – liquidation proceedings; Individuals or companies may file this chapter and assets are sold by a trustee. For businesses, the company ceases operation. Individuals receive a Discharge.

Chapter 7 Trustee – a person appointed in a Chapter 7 case to represent the interests of the bankruptcy estate and the unsecured creditors. Also known as the **Standing Trustee**.

Chapter 9 – bankruptcies of municipalities (government); only a few of these are filed each year.

Chapter 11 – reorganization proceedings, generally for business entities. The debtor maintains control of the business in Chapter 11, unless the Court appoints a trustee. Individuals can file Chapter 11 if they a very high amount of debt that exceeds the legal Debt Limits for Chapter 13.

Chapter 12 – family farmer bankruptcies. This was created by Congress in 1986 (Chapter 12 became effective on November 26, 1986). Only a family-owned farm business can qualify for Chapter 12 and it must have debt less than $1.5 million and have 50% of its income from farming operations.

Chapter 13 – bankruptcy proceedings for an individual with the intention of rescheduling the individual's debt (rather than liquidating the individual's assets and debt; an individual files under Chapter 7 to liquidate), Chapter 13 is referred to as wage earner bankruptcy, personal bankruptcy or consumer bankruptcy, Chapter 13 cannot be used by a partnership or a corporation; it can be used by a sole proprietorship. Chapter 13 allows a debtor to keep property and pay debts over time, usually three to five years. Also known as a **wage-earner bankruptcy**.

Chapter 13 Trustee – In Chapter 13, the office that administers the payment plans and keeps records of payments made by Chapter 13 Debtors. They assist the Judge with Confirmation of a Plan.

"Chapter 20" – an unofficial term describing the filing of a Chapter 7 proceeding followed by a Chapter 13. The Chapter 7 filing eliminates unsecured debts while the Chapter 13 filing handles continuing liens.

Claims – rights to repayment made by creditors against a debtor; they may be liquidated, unliquidated, fixed, contingent, matured, un-matured, secured, unsecured, subordinated, legal or equitable. (See **priority of claims.**)

Class – each of the different categories of claims against a debtor.

Complaint – the initiatory document in a lawsuit that notifies the court and the defendant of the grounds claimed by the Plaintiff for an award of money or other relief against the defendant.

Confirmation – the final approval by the bankruptcy court of a debtor's plan of reorganization. Confirmation takes place after resolution of any Objection by creditors.

Contested Matter – a dispute among the parties to a bankruptcy proceeding, instituted by the filing of a motion of the court.

Contingent Claim – a claim that may be owed by the debtor under certain circumstances. For example, where the debtor is a cosigner on another person's loan and that person fails to pay.

Conversion – changing chapters in bankruptcy (e.g., converting from Chapter 13 to Chapter 7).

Core Proceedings – those proceedings that are inherent in and fundamental to the administration of a bankruptcy case. Core proceedings are subject to the jurisdiction of the bankruptcy court. Non-core proceedings may be conducted outside the jurisdiction of the bankruptcy court.

Cram-down – confirmation of a plan of reorganization over the objections of one or more classes of creditors.

Creditor – a person to whom or business to which the debtor owes money or that claims to be owed money by the debtor.

Debts – money owed

Debt Negotiation (Workout or Credit Negotiation) – an arrangement, outside of bankruptcy, by a debtor and its creditors for payment or re-scheduling of payments of the debtor's obligations. Usually applies to an informal agreement between a business and its creditors, although it can be a formal agreement and it can also apply to consumer debtors and may be called.

Debtor – the entity seeking protection from creditors under the bankruptcy laws.

Default – the failure by an entity to abide by the covenants in a debt obligation or other agreement to which it is a party. The most common default is non-payment of interest or principal.

Discharge (of indebtedness) – the satisfaction or elimination of the debts of the debtor by the bankruptcy court.

Dischargeable debt – a debt for which the bankruptcy code allows the debtor's personal liability to be eliminated.

Discovery Procedures – used to obtain disclosure of evidence before trial.

Dismissal – the termination of a bankruptcy proceeding. The bankruptcy court can dismiss a case if it deems that the debtor or three creditors should not have filed or that a plan can never be formulated.

Docket – the schedule on which the clerk of the court records all motions, pleadings, memoranda, orders and all other court filings.

Effective Date – the date on which a plan of reorganization is implemented. It usually occurs after all the conditions to a plan of reorganization have been satisfied.

ECF or **Electronic Case Filing** – ECF is a comprehensive case management system that allows courts to maintain electronic case files and offer electronic filing over the Internet. Courts make all case information immediately available electronically through the Internet.

Equity – the value of the debtor's interest in property that remains after the liens and other creditor's interests are considered.

Executory Contract – a contract in which some or all of the obligations of each party have not yet been completed. The debtor-in-possession (or trustee) is allowed to reject unilaterally certain executory contracts.

Exemptions – laws that allow the protection of certain assets or properties owned by the debtor that cannot be recovered by creditors.

Filing Fees – The fee paid by the Debtor to the Court to file for Bankruptcy. Paid in addition to lawyer's fee.

First Meeting of Creditors (341 meeting) – a mandatory meeting between creditors and the debtor. It is usually held within a month of the filing of bankruptcy but often occurs later when the debtor has filed its schedules of financial information.

Fraudulent Conveyance – the transfer of valuable assets from a company which i) occurs when the company is technically insolvent, ii) renders the company insolvent, or iii) is made for less than adequate consideration. The spate of leveraged buyouts and other highly leveraged transactions in the 1980s has spurred a number of fraudulent conveyance allegations in recent years.

Fresh Start – informal term for the new accounting rules applicable to bankrupt companies. For companies that either filed for Chapter 11 after January 1991 or emerged from Chapter 11 after June 1991, assets are valued at market value rather than at historical cost.

Interim Order – a temporary order of the court pending a hearing, trial, a final order or while awaiting an act by one of the parties.

Lien – a charge upon a specific property designed to secure payment of a debt or performance of an obligation.

Liquidated Claim – a creditor's claim for a fixed amount of money.

Liquidation – the dissolution of a company, or individual; usually operations cease and assets are sold by auction; Chapter 7 is usually employed for liquidations, businesses or individuals.

Motion to Lift Automatic Stay – a request by a creditor to allow the creditor to take an action against a debtor or the debtor's property that would otherwise be prohibited by the automatic stay.

Non-Dischargeable Debt – a debt that cannot be eliminated in bankruptcy.

PACER (Public Access to Court Electronic Records) – a service provided by the court system that gives case filing information.

Party in Interest – a party who has standing to be heard by the court in a matter to be decided in the bankruptcy case. The debtor, the U.S. trustee or bankruptcy administrator, the case trustee and creditors are parties in interest for most matters.

Personal Bankruptcy – filed by an individual and also called a household bankruptcy, consumer bankruptcy or wage-earner bankruptcy. (see **Chapter 13** and also **Chapter 7**).

Petition – (or **bankruptcy petition** or **petition for relief**) - the document that commences a bankruptcy proceeding. Shorthand for bankruptcy petition, schedules (and plan in Chapter 13).

Petition Preparer – a business not authorized to practice law that prepares bankruptcy petitions.

Plan of Reorganization (Chapter 13 Plan) – the document setting forth how a bankrupt company plans to satisfy its creditors. The plan of reorganization is the cornerstone of a successful Chapter 11 bankruptcy.

Plaintiff – a person or business that files a Complaint in a court. In Bankruptcy the plaintiff will file an Adversary Complaint.

Post-Petition – the time *after* the filing date of a bankruptcy case.

Preference – a payment by a debtor made during a specified period (90 days or one year) prior to the filing that favors one creditor over others. Preference payments can usually be recovered and returned to the debtor's estate.

Pre-Petition – occurring before the filing date of a bankruptcy case.

Priority Claims – administrative expenses and salaries, wages, employee benefits, customer deposits and taxes which occurred pre-petition.

Pro Rata – proportionately per the size of the claim filed by the Creditor.

Proof of Claim – form filed by a creditor setting out its claims against a bankruptcy debtor.

Schedules – list submitted by the debtor along with the petition (or shortly thereafter) showing the debtor's assets, liabilities, and other financial information.

Secured Creditors – one of two general types of creditors of a company. Secured creditors have a lien on property of the company.

Secured Debt – debt backed by a mortgage, pledge of collateral or other lien. It is debt for which the creditor has the right to pursue specific pledged property upon default.

Set-off – the ability to discharge or reduce a debt by applying a counter claim between the same parties. For example, a bank which has lent money to a debtor may attempt to satisfy some or all of the loan by seizing the debtor's deposits at the bank.

Straight Bankruptcy – an informal term for a Chapter 7 bankruptcy or liquidation; used more commonly to describe liquidation before the Bankruptcy Reform Act of 1978.

Substantial Abuse – a term that refers to the abuse of the privilege to file a petition. It usually describes fraud in cases of personal bankruptcy.

Trustee – an agent of the court who manages the property of the debtor for the benefit of the creditors. The court appoints a trustee in most Chapter 7 cases and in Chapter 11 cases when it determines that the debtor's management should not remain in their control. This type of trustee should be distinguished from the **U.S. Trustee**, who plays an administrative role in all bankruptcy cases.

United States Trustee – an agent of the U.S. Department of Justice appointed to assist in bankruptcy cases. The U.S. Trustee administers many of the duties of the court including appointing committees, appointing trustees and examiners, scrutinizing bankruptcy documents, etc.

Unsecured Claim – a claim or debt for which a creditor holds no special assurance of payment; a debt for which credit was extended based solely upon the creditor's assessment of the debtor's future ability to pay.

Unsecured Creditor – a creditor who extended credit to a debtor without collateral security. If the debtor files for bankruptcy or is levied upon, the unsecured creditors are paid on a pro-rata basis only after the claims of all secured creditors are satisfied.

Unliquidated Claim – a claim for which a specific value has not been determined.

Voluntary Bankruptcy – bankruptcy filed by the debtor him or herself. Almost all bankruptcies are Voluntary Bankruptcies.

Made in the USA
Monee, IL
05 November 2026

67790723R00046